# AETERNITAS

# Aeternitas

## Trista Woojin

Trista Woojin

First of all, thank you for purchasing "Aeternitas." I honestly did not think anyone would bother doing so; therefore, it sort of blows my mind to know that this book is now in someone else's hands. It's a very strange thought and one that I have not managed to wrap my mind around just yet.

It is of absolutely no importance, but note that "Aeternitas" has been revised; the previous version was exceptionally misprinted, which was something I only noticed when I received my own printed copies. So, the reason this book had been delayed in reaching its destination is not that it decided to fuck off toward parts unknown, but because I had to edit it and submit revisions.

That being said, I do have to admit that being published is a very strange thing. I'm honestly not sure if the shock and wondering "what kind of dumpster-fire spewing fresh hell did I just unleash on the world?!" will ever stop, but that's kind of beside the point.

### DISCLAIMER

Though you will not read profanity in the verses contained within this tome, certain individuals may take exception to, or be offended by, some of the subject matter.

The questionable content you will encounter includes, but is not limited to: Fantasy (including magic, monsters and rituals,) non-explicit murder, hellish carnivals, moral greyness, sarcasm, coffeeshop-style verse, poetic pretentiousness, sarcasm, satire, casual nihilism, self-mockery, living puppets, supernatural horror, cosmic horror, poetic criticisms of government and war, as well as verses that may call the reader to just think about what they are reading.

If you happen to experience perplexity, discomfort, disillusionment, disgust, anger, carpal tunnel, hair loss, sweaty palms, blurry vision, the ability to speak in Eldritch tongues, the ability to see through time itself, lycanthropy, nausea, heartburn, indigestion, upset stomach and diarrhea, then you are advised to seek out the assistance of a young priest and an old priest.

The poetry contained within this book is nothing more than fiction. Should it bear a resemblance to anything in the real world, that is merely a coincidence.

# I

# We've Been Trying To Reach You

A hellish message whispers through the air
"We've been trying to reach you concerning
your vehicle's extended warranty"
"You should've received a notice in the mail
about your car's extended warranty eligibility"

But the letter remains unread,
lost in a sea of forgotten papers
As the calls persist, a relentless drone
in the depths of despair

"Since we've not gotten response,
we're giving you a final courtesy call"
A warning, a threat, a promise of impending doom

Press 2 to be removed,
to escape the clutches of this spectral call
To be placed on a do-not-call list,
a sanctuary in a world of darkness

Yet the temptation lingers, a siren's song calling
out with deceitful allure
To speak to someone about possibly
extending or reinstating your vehicle's warranty
Press 1 to speak with a warranty specialist,

a whispered promise of salvation
But what price must be paid,
what horrors await in the depths of this unholy bargain?
A contract sealed in blood,
a pact with forces beyond comprehension

# II

# Resilience of Forgotten Dreams

Once a vibrant city stood, full of life and cheer,
Now just a ghostly ruin, abandoned and austere.
Through empty streets I tread, where the echoes softly weep,
Where shadows long to speak, and lost memories seep.
Once long ago, laughter filled this place,
Fairy tales were woven through each cobbled space.
But now the buildings crumble, their timbers worn and frayed,
Nature reclaims her throne, as man's creation fades

A doleful hush befalls, upon this forsaken town,
As if even the wind dare not disturb its mournful frown.
The remnants of life's stories, whisper in each gust,
Tales of love and loss, now left to rot and rust.

The silence hangs heavy, like a shroud upon my soul,
With every labored step, deeper into shadows
I stroll. Oh, what tragedy befell, to leave such a scarred affray,
To extinguish the flame, and let darkness hold its sway.
Perhaps it was a war, with hatred as its fuel,
Consuming hope and dreams, in its relentless duel.
Or maybe plagues arose, spreading like a poisoned vine,

Taking lives and futures, spilled like bitter wine.
But hidden in the desolation, a haunting beauty lies,
An elegy of the past, written in ruins and empty skies,
The way the ivy climbs, caressing ancient stones,
Seems to whisper secrets, only the wind condones.

In each abandoned doorway, phantoms seem to dwell,
Figures from forgotten days, trapped in a ghostly spell.
They dance in moonlit shadows, to a melody unsung,
The creaking of the wooden beams, like whispers in the
night,
As if the very buildings weep, beneath pale moon's soft light.
Their crumbling architecture, a testament to lost grace,
Yet their skeletal frames still hold memories in their embrace.

I see a broken window, its shards reflecting stars,
A glimpse of lives once lived, now hidden behind scars.
Who were the souls that dwelt here, in fleeting mortal coil?
What dreams did they pursue, what secrets did they toil?
Something stirs within me, a sorrow for the lost,
For dreams once held so dear, now abandoned and tossed.

But within this melancholy, a sense of solace lies,
For in this desolation, rebirth can arise.

Through the crumbling city streets, a new world breathes anew,
As nature reclaims its rightful place, beneath the sky's vast blue.
And though the silence deafens, and the ghosts still linger here,
he memory of what once was, forever shall persevere.
There exists a haunting beauty, in the depths of sorrow's glow.
As I walk these abandoned streets,
I am reminded of the fragility of existence,
Of the ephemeral nature of all things,
And the resilience of forgotten dreams.

# III

## Oathbound

In lands where darkness shrouds the sun,
Where tortured souls forever run,
A world defined by broken oaths,
And whispers bound by spectral cloths.
In this realm of forgotten vows,
Where emptiness now creeps and prowls,
Each broken promise, a heavy stone,
Leaves ghostly traces all alone.
Where dreams hide and hope meets its doom,
Where promises broken unleash a haunting snare.

For every vow whispered with a tender plea,
The weight of unfulfilled commitment bleeds,
Promises, both grand and minuscule,
Leave spectral traces, dark and cruel.
In this land of forgotten oaths,

Ghosts of words roam like spectral cloths,
Each whisper, each vow, each solemn pledge,
Binds the promise-giver with surrender's edge.

They sway through the night with mournful cries,

Phantoms of commitments lost to lies,
Their ethereal forms echo through the air,
Desolate whispers of regret and despair.
From the smallest pledge to the grandest vow,
Unkept words haunt the here and now,
They cling to hearts like chains of lead,
A chorus of regrets, a future, dead.

For every lover sworn to be true,
Whose hollow words like arrows flew,
Their ghostly remnants linger still,
Aching hearts forever left to fill.
In eyes that once held hopes so bright,
Now lingers only endless night,
Love's promise turned to shattered glass,
Leaving only echoes of the past.

And what of dreams, so grand and vast,
That wither like flowers, fading fast?
Each abandoned wish like a beacon's flare,
Now lost in a labyrinth of despair.
For every dreamer who dared to soar,
But found their wings forever tore

Their spectral presence wanders free,
Aching for the heights they'll never see.
In homes where childhood laughter thrived,
But love and care somehow contrived,
To dissolve into bitter strife,
Leaving broken hearts like shards of life.

The weight of failed guidance carries on,
In burdens that can never be undone.
Oh, wells of promises, empty and vast,
Each broken word built to forever last,

From whispered secrets to solemn oaths,
Every unkept pledge a haunting ghost.

And as these specters haunt the night,
They beg for redemption, for what is right,
For those who uttered words unkind,
To feel the weight they left behind.

From personal vows to the grandest schemes,
The world is blanketed in spectral gleams,
Each broken promise a solemn reminder,
Of souls entangled in eternal binders.
So ponder well before you speak,
Lest your words become the ghosts that creep,
Through the hearts and minds of those who hear,
Forever shaping the atmosphere.

For in this world where oaths are spun,
And broken promises are never undone,
Each spectral echo weaves its tale,
Of lives entangled, lost in its wail.
May we learn the weight of each word we choose,
To honor the promises we cannot lose,
We're bound forever to our words alone

# IV

# Hell's Circus

The fear in my gut grew as the laughter got louder,
In this cursed circus, where darkness knew no bound,
A macabre menagerie, blood-stained and forever coward,
I stood, a spectator lost, in madness profound.
Beneath a moonless sky, an ominous tent stood,
Its canvas black as the whispers of the damned,
There dwelled the demented, the wicked and crude,
In this twisted realm where innocence was condemned.

As the stars trembled above, casting feeble light,
A haunting wind whispered tales of woe and despair,
A carnival of shadows emerged from the stygian night,
Where cotton candy was bloodied,
And balloons filled with nightmares.
I dared to venture forth, amid lurking trepidation,
Engulfed by a curiosity unwise,

For behind that black veil, my soul's liberation,
Unleashed an abyss, where the wicked thrive.

The clowns, with painted grins, bore wicked intentions,
Their eyes, the windows to a darkness untold,
Malevolence oozed through their devilish inventions,
Twisted smiles, hiding secrets of malice unfold.
Gleaming knives glinted, concealed beneath robes of bright
hue,
Jugglers, dancing on razors, with a sinister zeal,
Their graceful movements masked what horrors they could
do,
A ballet of bloodshed, chaos they'd so brilliantly unveil.

Acrobats leapt through the air like vengeful spirits,
Twisted contortionists twisted into monstrous shapes,
And high above, the trapeze played on intentions malign,
Each act a macabre masterpiece, veiled by grim escapes.
The ringmaster, a master of deceit, with eyes of icicle blue,
His voice, a lethal melody, a siren's dark embrace,
He summoned his minions to the sinister debut,
Binding their souls to this malevolent circus in disgrace.
The tightrope walker danced precariously on a precipice,
Her delicate balance a cruel metaphor for life,
With each agonizing step, she teetered on the edge of abyss,
Summoning terrors beneath a tattered veil of strife.
v
The lion tamer commanded the wild beasts' ethereal growls,
Their eyes alight with hidden fire and despair,

From their iron teeth, darkness seeped, ensnaring souls,
Their roars echoed the cries of the helpless, the ensnared.
Beneath a cracked spotlight, the juggler's knives did gleam,
Moonlight danced upon the edge of gleaming steel,
As lifeless bodies fell

# V

# Celestial Lullaby

Beneath the cloak of night, a shadowy choir,
Stars in the abyss, their voices dire.
Ancient light weaves a cosmic shroud,
Whispers of mysteries, where darkness is endowed.

In the starry tapestry, secrets unfold,
A celestial chorus of stories untold.
Echoes of eons in each haunting strain,
A cosmic lament, a celestial pain.

They sing of worlds long turned to dust,
Of galaxies colliding, in chaos thrust.
Their cosmic whispers, a haunting hymn,
In the vast emptiness, where shadows swim.
A symphony of blackness, a cosmic plea,
Stars in the void, singing eerily.

Messages coded in the language of night,
Revealing the secrets, the universe's fright.

Listen closely, and you'll hear the cries,

Of dying stars in the cosmic skies.
A dance of shadows, a spectral trance,
As the stars' chorus weaves its dark romance.

The human soul, a captive to their song,
Awe and terror, a duality strong.
In the echoes of their melancholic croon,
Lies the cosmic wisdom of an ancient moon.

What might we learn if we heed their call,
In the abyss where the starlight falls?
A communion with the void, a spectral dance,
As the stars' chorus weaves its dark expanse.

# VI

# Lost Lexicon

A language lost, a cadence caught in time's slow sand,
A once binding melody that graced the land.
This was the speech of soul to soul, a bridge across the minds,
A symphony of shared life, now mute, the tapestry unwinds.
It wove a common narrative, a thread through every heart,
Now frayed and faded, torn apart, its speakers long depart.

It whispered in the rustling leaves and in the flowing streams,
A dialect of unity, of shared collective dreams.
With every word a brushstroke on the canvas of our kin,
A picture painted deeply with the hues of where we've been.
But silence fell, like evening's cloak, upon this gentle sound,
And with it took the common ground where our spirits once were found.
In its absence, a hollow void, a gap we cannot breach,
A language lost to modern lips, a shore we cannot reach.

The beauty of its mystery, like mist upon the dawn,
A memory of the language that the world has since
withdrawn. It spoke of deeper things than can be captured
by the word,
A music felt within the chest, more felt than it was heard.
Its speakers knew a harmony, a bond through spoken spell,
A connection deeper than the tales that any voice could tell.
Now echoes in the chambers of the ancients' hallowed halls,
A ghost of language haunting still the memory that calls.

Rediscovery, a yearning quest, to find what's been misplaced,
To touch the remnants of a past that time has all but erased.
A hope to resurrect the chords of a forgotten tune,
To sing once more the anthem of a world that's out of tune.
For in that lost language lies the essence of our past,
A key to unlock wisdom that the ages have amassed.
To find again the words that once defined our very being,
Could bring us back to wholeness, a new way of seeing.

The resonance of lost words, the power they possess,
To heal our fractured world, and our brokenness address.
To speak again the language that once made us all as one,
To rediscover harmony, and a new day begun.
But until that day, we mourn the loss, the silence left behind,
A void where once was music that could harmonize mankind.
The forgotten language, a testament to all that's come and
gone,
A reminder of the unity we've lost, yet still long on.

# VII

# Cantata Nihil

Where echoes of the not-done, softly die,
I tread with feet that drag the weight of never,
Through the winding ways of a relentless ever.

The walls, a gallery of ghosts unbidden,
Portraits of the past, in the present hidden,
Each corridor, a chronicle of chances lost,
A labyrinth laid with the stones of yore,
A mosaic of moments, that are no more.

Each turn, a testament to time's cruel knack,
For painting futures that will never crack,
The surface of now, the veneer of here,
The ever-unchanging, the always-near.

This maze, a mind's own making, a heart's own heft,

A place where the weft of life is left,
Unwoven, threads dangling, in disarray,
A tapestry of choices, frayed.
No Minotaur awaits, no beast to best,
Just the winding paths of the unexpressed,

A prison, yes, but also a retreat,
A place where the pulse of potential beats.

The silence hums with the songs unsung,
With the bells unrung, with the leaps unlunged,
Each step, a story stillborn, unspun,
A dance of shadow, 'neath the unseen sun.
Unpatterned, unsorted, unsought,
The labyrinth, a landscape of the soul's own strife,

A map of the maze that is life.

Sanctuary in the solitude of self,
Where the 'could-have-been' books line the shelf
, In this quiet cloister of the could,
Where the echoes of the undone brood.
A wandering through the weald of woe,
A seeking in the silt, a longing to know,
Why each path not taken, each turn not made,
Each silent echo, each memory unplayed.

The labyrinth holds, within its twist and twine,
The essence of the ever-divine,

The mortal coil, the eternal question,
The undying quest for life's own lesson.

In the shattered refrain, there is beauty, there is pain,
A symphony of solitude, a solitary refrain,
The wandering soul in the labyrinth lies,
Captured in the space between the earth and skies.

Through the meandering maze of mind, T
he exit sought, but not to find,
For in the journey is the worth,
The labyrinth, a mirror of our birth.

So roam I do, through the snaking snare,
Each choice not taken, a silent prayer,
A wish for the roads that went untread,
A lament for the life that lies undead.
Both prison and sanctuary, this maze I roam,
In the labyrinth of regret, I find my home,
A place to ponder, to pause, to peer,

Into the depths of the self, so near, so dear.

In the hush of twilight's final gleaming,
A cadence creeps, through the air it's streaming,
A symphony of ruin, a dirge so profound,
Where desolation's breath is the only sound.

The maestro is time, with merciless hand,

Conducting the fall of a once vibrant land.
The baton she wields is invisible, cold,
Turning cities to stories, untold and old.

First, the strings of the weeping willows play,
Sighing for the souls that have wandered away.
Their mournful tunes weave through shattered halls,
Where laughter once echoed, now silence befalls.

The percussion, a slow and unyielding drone,
Of crumbling stone upon ancient bone.
The timpani of thunder, a roof caving in,
The final collapse, a deafening din.

The woodwinds are whispers of movements unseen,
The rustling of leaves, where man has been.
A flute's soft lament for what's been erased,
A clarinet's cry for the beauty defaced.

The brass bellows deep with the winds' wild roar,
Through the hollowed remnants of the days of yore.
A trumpet's blare in the dead of night,
A horn's long call, seeking the light.

The chorus, a haunting echo of loss,
The eerie refrain of nature's emboss.

Vines that strangle the life they adorn,
Reclaiming the land, both mourned and reborn.

Pianissimo, the sound of a drop,
The leakage of time, it never does stop.
The patter of rain on a rusted-out car,
A melody playing to the evening star.

And there, in the dark, the softest of drums,
The heartbeat of earth, as the end comes.
It throbs in the ground, a subtle quake,
In the symphony of ruin, in the wake.
In the world where the shadows of despair fall.
For within the decay, and the sorrow, and fears,
Lies the music of ages, the song that endures the endless years

# VIII

# Whispers of the Abyss

A chasm not of earth and stone,
But the darkest echoes, where fears are sown.
The human experience, a labyrinth vast,
In the abyss, the shadows cast.

Despair, a silent wail, a haunting cry,
Lost within the recesses of a troubled sky.
The whispers tell of sorrow's art,
A canvas painted with a broken heart.
Loss echoes through the hollow air,
A symphony of grief, a weight to bear.
Unexplored depths of the psyche's domain,
Where secrets dwell, and fears remain.

Listen, as the abyss unveils its lore,
A narrative of anguish, forevermore.

In the corners where darkness breeds,
The whispers dance to forbidden creeds.

Reveal the secrets, the silent screams,
Unveil the nightmares from fractured dreams.

The abyss speaks of the human plight,
A tapestry woven in the veils of night.

Expressing fears that linger and twine,
In the labyrinth of thoughts, a complex design.
As you stand on the edge, the whispers rise,
Echoing the shadows that within us lies.

A paradoxical dance, a mysterious trance,
The abyss speaks, giving voice to chance.
For in the darkest corners of the mind,
The whispers of the abyss, a truth to find.

# IX

# River of Lost Time

Lost within the depths of time, a river does flow,
Carrying stories, whispered long ago.
Lost, overlooked, or silenced by fate,
They dance in currents, an eternal debate.

This river, a vessel for forgotten tales,
Mingling and intertwining, as memory fails.
Each story a fragment, a glimpse, a trace,
Bound by the river's relentless embrace.
The river's waters, a tapestry of old,
Where history and memory fiercely unfold.
For what is remembered shapes our past,
While what is forgotten fades into shadows cast.

Oh, the journey to seek these submerged lore,
To dive into depths never explored before.

To unearth the narratives hidden from sight,
And voice the voices silenced in the night.

Beneath the surface, secrets lie in wait,
Whispering truths, defying the hands of fate.

They speak of triumphs, of battles fought,
Of love and loss, lessons hard-won and taught.

The river's current, an ancient guide,
Leading through time, where the forgotten reside.
And as I navigate this watery domain,
I hear the echoes of stories, a haunting refrain.

I hear the voice of a nameless hero,
Whose valor was lost, yet refuses to zero.
I hear the laughter of forgotten lovers
, Their passion a flame that time smothers.

I hear the cries of the oppressed and oppressed,
Their struggles and triumphs, forever impressed. I
hear the dreams of those who dared to dream,
Their visions still vibrant, though silenced it seems.

These submerged narratives, they long to be heard,
To break free from the river, like a soaring bird.
They yearn for recognition, for their truths to be known,
To reclaim their place in history's grand throne.
So, I'll journey on, through this river of time,

Unearthing the stories, no longer confined.
And as I give voice to the forgotten and lost,
Their tales will rise, no matter the cost.

# X

# Anemone

On the knife-edge of fear, I stand alone,
In the darkest corner of this barren throne,
Where shadows dance, in eternal levitation
And light is a myth, a cursed abomination
And like an ember, flickering in the night

Hope teeters, a fragile existence, in flight,
As darkness consumes, and heartbeats falter,
A symphony of despair, a haunting Psalter.
Beyond the horizon, where nightmares breed,
Silent echoes whisper, sprouting like a seed
A desolate landscape of forgotten dreams,
Where reality twists, tearing at the seams.
In this forsaken realm, where sanity mends,
Visions of desolation claw at the bends,
Where broken souls wander, lost and forlorn

Seeking solace in a world bleak and torn.
Above, the sky weeps, with bloodied tears,
A lamentation for the pain endured for years,

Anchored to the earth, burdened with sorrow
The sun no longer rises, no hope of tomorrow.

Intertwined with despair, a paradoxical woe,
Like a phoenix rising, determined to grow,
You, an ethereal traveler, trapped in this tale,
Bearing scars and secrets, a vulnerable scale.
And in this darkness, your essence blooms
Like an anemone, weathered, yet it assumes,
A delicate beauty, a resilience unseen,
In this barren wasteland, you reign supreme.
The world may tremble, under despair's trance,
But you, unyielding, in your daring dance

Embrace the shadows with your fiery might,
Igniting your soul in the depths of this night
, On the knife-edge of fear, you take a stance,
Defying the darkness with every chance,
For in the depths of this unforgiving land,
You bloom, strong, an anemone's ethereal strand.

# XI

# Hope For A Fading World

A world once bathed in golden hues of morn,
Now tangled in lament, in anguish it is torn.
For light is fading, both in soul and sight,
And hope within the depths begins to take its flight.
Across the land, a mournful hush descends,
Once a realm of radiant dreams and sacred bliss,
Now shrouded by the weight of sorrow's kiss.
The ethereal glow, once their guide,
Dissolves to nothingness, leaving them to decide,
How to cope with the gradual descent,
Into a realm where light appears to be spent.

In this growing darkness, spirits falter,
Candles of joy flicker, and hope begins to alter.

Hearts once vibrant, eager, fierce, and bold,
Now bear the weight of stories yet untold.
For love has waned and lost its tender glow,
A casualty of a world forever cloaked in woe.
And the moon itself, its luminescence fade,
As tears uncounted fall in a silent cascade.

The dwellers of this realm tread paths of gloom,
As they grapple with sorrow, seeking to exhume
The remnants of a time when laughter reigned,
When angels danced and love was unrestrained.
But now they dwell in a state numbed by despair,
Their souls entwined in a ceaseless snare,
As darkness creeps with its malevolent gait,
Draining their spirits, sealing their fate.

Yet In this bleak and somber guise,
Some persevere, refusing to close their eyes.
They clutch at flickering rays of fading light,
Determined to banish darkness with all their might.
In whispered hushed tones and defiant cries,
They speak of legends, of forgotten skies,
Of an era where light beamed strong and bright,
And love fought valiantly, vanquishing the night.

They gather in secret, in hidden groves
, And sing ancient hymns to the stars above,
Seeking solace in memories and tales of old,
For in those stories, hope begins to unfold.

Though the world may seem lost, mired in despair,
In their hearts, a spark remains, a flame so rare,
And with every flicker, they vow to ignite,
A revolution against darkness, a valiant fight.

For in the depths of sorrow, there lies a seed,
A seed of courage, of resilience, indeed.
And from the embers of fading light's reign,
New heroes arise, their destiny to reclaim.
They rise, with blades unsheathed, and hearts on fire,
To kindle the passion that darkness may conspire

, To bring forth a future with hope as its might,
And bathe the world once more in radiant light.

Though shadows may lengthen, and troubles persist,
The struggle against darkness they simply cannot resist.
United they stand, a force unyielding and bold,
Together they walk, the brave and the uncontrolled.
For in this land where light slowly fades,
Hope finds a way, sheltered in whispered serenades,
In the symphony of hearts intertwining,
A testament of resilience, forever shining.

So let us remember, as the light grows dim,
That even in darkness, we've the strength within.
To rise, to ignite, to fiercely defy,
The looming terrors as they pass us by.
For as long as one voice echoes with might,

The world may yet awaken from perpetual night,
And despite the fading light, we shall find,
An unwritten tale of hope, forever enshrined.

# XII

# Rafflesia

Blood drips, staining sands once lush with life,
Nightmare's shadows haunt, death's grip so tight.
Humanity once thrived, but now no more,
Not a single tear from what was before.
Black sky ablaze with lightning's twisted dance,
Flames devour the wilted, forsaken plants.
No sign of life, not even a flicker of breath,
This empty land echoes hatred and death.

Beneath the blood-red moon's seductive glare,
A solitary creature emerges, dark and rare.
Innocence's blood stains her trembling hands,
She straddles the line between two forsaken lands.
Where the living roam and the dead reside,
Grinning wickedly, her power amplified.
A field of death, her pride and her domain,

Mindless beings slain, silenced with disdain.
Summoned by fools who sought their desires,
Blind to the impending doom, consumed by fires.
They offered their souls, their fates were sealed,
Unaware, they bowed to her, unaware they kneeled.

She gazes upon the beheaded, the lifeless forms,
Charred skeletons scattered, as darkness transforms.
Sighing contently, her heart filled with glee,
Destruction herself, summoned by their decree.

# For Those Who Wander

The world has lost its grip on sanity's reign,
As illusions dance, weaving a wicked chain.
The government, once a beacon of control,
Now tumbles down a rabbit hole,
Madness seeps through distorted veins,
While truth dissolves within deceit's remains.

Twisted lands, embellished in deceptive guise,
Truths buried deep, covered by disguise,
Their treacherous veils of words and untruth,
Stealing hopes, extinguishing dreams of youth.
Unheeding the people's anguished cries,
As innocence fades and hope slowly dies
, In darkened chambers, they plead and plea,
But winds carry their voices, unheard and free.

Falling now as empires, lost to time's decay,
Their grandeur and glory, mere echoes, they sway,
Crumbled monuments witness the ages' swift bend,
While echoes of anguish cry out, refusing to end.

Gladiators emerge from the depths of despair,
Wearing scars like crowns, their eyes ablaze with a glare
, They rise from shadows, fueled by wrath and rage,
Determined to break free from this twisted cage.

Come, wanderer, step into this ethereal abyss,
Witness illusions blend with reality's hiss,
In this realm where darkness strokes the midnight sky,
Stay by my side as the world starts to bid goodbye.

Together, we'll explore the realms of twisted dreams,
Uncover secrets hidden within despair's seams,
In haunting depths where hope intertwines,
Our souls entwined, transcending earthly confines.
Inviting you to taste the bitter nectar of mystic pain,
As haunting melodies play, dancing in the rain,
We'll wander through the veils, where shadows blend,
And kindle a fire that burns, refusing its end.

Ethereal whispers shall guide us through the night,
As we navigate the labyrinth of this phantasmal plight,
For in darkness, beauty often lies concealed

# XIII

# The Lost

I met you last night a thousand years ago,
In the shadows where sorrow does sow.
At the intersection of dreams and reality,
Where lost souls wander in eternal calamity.
Beneath the moon's lament and starry sky,
Where time stands still, suspended, passing by,
There, where cotton candy foxgloves gleam,
I entered a realm where nightmares teem.

In this twisted realm, where hope entwines,
All possible worlds are born but to decline,
They bloom like flowers touched by decay,
Withering, fading, as life ebbs away.

We stood outside the rusted tower gates,
Entrapped in an illusion our fate dictates,

Unseen by the cruel destinies that scheme,
Locked in a dance, to an ancient theme.
Spoken words echoed through that broken hour,
As we conversed on the ledge of a sorrowful tower,
Yet, our voices were whispers, fleeting and frail,
Lost, like desperate pleas adrift in the gale.

Then, your ghostly figure whispered to me,
Those words, oh so cruel, as venomous as can be,
"You are not real, just a specter like me,
Trapped in this world with no chance to be free."
And as you turned and walked away,
Your voice faded, becoming fragments, austere,
Like ashes on the wind, carried on a sorrowful breath,
Leaving me stranded, alone, in a land of imminent death.

Now, with each passing night, I search in vain,
For the dream that tethered us, destiny's bane,,
Whispering your name into the shadows.
For in that fleeting moment, a thousand years hence,
So I wander through the darkness and despair,
Haunted by memories that refuse to decay

# XIV

# Shackles of the Dreamer

Yesterday I saw the sun go black,
A chilling omen of impending doom,
The rays entwined with shadows, soulless,
And watched the sky turn ruby-red, a tomb.
The voices of the damned began to sing,
A haunting chorus upon the hollow wind,
Their wicked incantations pierced my ears,
A chilling, broken echo of sins never committed.

I watched the oceans turn to dust,
Their salty waves transformed to sand,
Beneath my feet, the earth crumbled,
As smoke billowed from the ground, a wicked brand.
Last night I watched the stars collide,

Celestial bodies crashing, cosmic strife,

As the moon slunk from her stage,

A lost performer, fleeing from her life.

The counterfeit worlds began to collapse,

Illusions shattered, broken dreams,

Reality, like fragile threads unwound,

And dreams emerged, a terrifying theme.

As your ghost crashed into me,

A specter of that should have been,

How could you believe in me,

When I am nothing?

How could I be anything at all,

When all words are empty and hollow?

Bound by darkness, we are but a shade,

In this sinister realm where shadows swallow.

This morning, I woke from the dream,

To find all worlds crumbling, hope unfound,

Waiting for some miracle, ephemeral,

I saw the cryptic visions all around.

I heard the mournful cries of ghosts,

Trapped in the realms beyond our sight,

Danced with eternity as the symphony screamed,

A macabre ballet, a ghostly night.

And in this twisted dance of fate,

I learned we are nothing but a cosmic joke,

Puppets in the hands of unseen forces,

Forever yearning, forever broke.

# Dream-snare

Beware the venomous arachnid queen,
Surfacing from her astral demesne.
Within the mind's labyrinth, she awakes,
A predator, her quarry she forsakes.
Boundless webs enshroud her domain,
Engulfing sleepers in her cryptic reign.
Through the tapestry veiled in darkest lore,
She hunts her prey forevermore.

Patient hunter, her eyes infernal,
A flameless fire, glistening eternal.
In ethereal realms, she stalks with glee,

Her victim's dreams her necropolis key.
Through reverie's portals, she dances free,
A dervish of shadows and mystery.

In visions tainted by venomous thrums,
She weaves her fate, her purpose becomes.
Whispers of ruin through slumber's cloth,
She devours nocturnal visions, raw and froth.
Her fangs drip poison's malevolent curse,
Infecting dreams with a venomous verse.
Labyrinthine paths, woven with deceit,
Lost souls wander, ensnared, incomplete.
Every step leads closer, captive's doom,
Drowning in nightmares' arcane bloom.

Awakening minds shrouded in dread,
Haunted by memories, silently fled.
The spider's presence, a looming blight,
A nightmare's touch, everlasting delight.
Oh, hapless dreamer, unaware you may be,
A spider's prey, bound in webs you can't see.
Within slumber's realm, she tightens her hold,
Your dreams consumed, secrets to unfold.
A monstrous union, dream and night collide,
In this dance, no secrets can hide.

# XVI

# The Poisoned Harvest

In shadows clad with murky guise,
A twisted tale I must devise,
Where poison's essence taints the air
And minds, corrupted, now ensnared.
Leaders emerge, their motives veiled,
To mire the truth-- as truth, curtailed.
From halls of power, deceit unfurls,

A harvest vast, of minds in swirls,
They sow illusions, feed us lies,
While poisoning our thoughts, as spies.
Like puppeteers with silver strings,
They lead the dance, controlling kings,
Each thought usurped, a puppet's dance,
Capturing minds in their vile trance.

They prey on masses, longing souls,
Convincing them they need their roles,
A cage of shackles tightly bound,
With poisoned thoughts, their minds are drowned.

A throbbing wave of cruel intent,
They whisper falsehoods, discontent,
Stealing truth, as harvest, ripe
See how they sow, from twisted loom,
Their cultivated, darkened gloom,
Divide and conquer, their grand scheme,
To break the unity of a forgotten dream.
Their poison spreads, like venomous vine,
Through webs of twisted, gnarled design,
From echoes of despair they feast,
On minds of those desperately seeking peace.

But still, a glimmer of hope resides,
Among the ones whom freedom guides,
To break the chains, their minds unbind
And rend the darkness, shattering blind.
Awaken, masses, from slumber deep,
Question authority, secrets seek,
Unshackle thoughts, embrace the light,
Thwart the harvest, and end the blight.

# XVII

# The Watcher

A ghostly Watcher lurks, bereaved.
In depths of darkness, she awaits,
In corners dim, where time abates.
Beneath the moon, her pallid guise,
Cryptic whispers drown out her cries.
Her spectral form, a wretched sight,
Haunting souls lost in endless night.

In eerie realms of twisted dreams,
Her haunting presence ever teems.
She wanders through the misty gloom,
In somber aura, dread consumes.
The Watcher, veiled in shades of grey,
Obscured, eluding light of day.
Her eyes two hollow wells,
Reflections of desolate spells.

Far from the realm of mortal might,
Her spirit dances in twilight.
With every breath from unseen lips,
A haunting echo of dark crypts.
She seeks abandoned, forlorn spaces,
In crumbling walls of broken grace,
She finds solace in the ghostly chase.
The Watcher's gaze can pierce the veil,
Unseen to mortal eyes that fail.
She sees the darkness they dismiss,
Their tainted essence, their secret bliss.
Within the dank and lifeless halls,
The Watcher weaves her haunting thralls.
Her whispers coil, a twisted blade,
To tempt the lost, the hearts decayed.
She feeds on fear, indulges lust,
A spectral dance, her wicked thrust.
With every breath, she grips her prey,
Freezing souls in eternal gray.
Her whispers, soft, yet venomous,
Conceal her twisted double fuss.
For in her game of mounting dread,
She revels in the thrill, undead.
The Watcher's cunning, cruel design
, To wait and watch, no light to shine.
In corners deep, she'll hide and stay,
Until the last of life will sway.
So heed this caution, mortal wight,

Lest you invite her baleful sight.
For in the corners, dark and blight,
The Watcher waits, forever night.

# XVIII

# The Blight

In the shadows where darkness breeds,
A twisted tale of human deeds,
I'll spin a verse untamed and raw,
Of how we are the world's cruel flaw.
From deepest depths, a sickness looms,
A pestilence with countless tombs,
Within our hearts, a void of light,
As we unleash eternal night.

We grasp at treasures, wealth untold,
But leave destruction in our hold,
Like locusts swarming, we devour,
Every leaf, every vibrant flower.
With poisoned tongues and greedy eyes,
We bring destruction to the skies,
Tainting waters, ravaging land,

Leaving barren a once fertile sand.

The creatures we were meant to share,
We hunt and maim without a care,
Their sacred essence lost and gone,

Their mournful cries forever spawn.
Humanity, a vile parasite,
Feeding on the world's fading light
, Our ego sprawled, our arrogance clear,
As we manipulate, pollute, and leer.

We wear our masks, deceive and pry,
While mother nature's children die,
We calculate our selfish gain,
As innocent lives shriek in pain.
Our swords are bathed in crimson stain,
As we wage war for personal gain,
Avarice, hatred, devoid of grace,
In this desolate and twisted place.

The forests weep, their tears run dry,
As we sever limbs, let forests die,
The ocean's breathe grows short and weak,
As we exploit, relentless and bleak.
But hear me now, you wretched lot,
For devastation's what we've brought,
The world, once pure, now deeply scarred,
By human hands, forever marred.

In twisted rhyme, my words unfold,
The unrelenting truth, behold,
That humankind in all its might,
Is nothing but the cruelest blight.

# XIX

# Transformation and Reclamation

From the twisted bowels of nature's embrace,
Emerges a darkness, a vile disgrace,
Creatures once pure, imbued with malice,
Transformed by the blast, their souls callous.
The wails of the dying trees linger in the air,
Stifled by the stench of death's despair,
No birdsong greets the morn, no life blooms,
Only twisted creatures now roam, In doom.

Behold the forest's eyes, once gentle and wise,
Now pierced with crimson fervor, their spirit dies,
Where bunnies gambled, now darkened shadows thrive,
A sly, blood-thirsty gleam within each eye.
Ravens once cawed with solemn, eerie grace,

Now soar with menace, spreading chaos they embrace,
Their cries unravel the souls of those who hear,
A haunting symphony of malevolence and fear.

The wolves, once noble with moonlit grace,
Are now nocturnal predators, a savage race,
With teeth like daggers, their hunger fierce,
No mercy shown, only instinct's fierce pierce.
In the depths of rivers, where serpents slumber,
Now monstrous leviathans weave and lumber,
With slimy scales and fangs dripping venom's flow,
They hunt the unwary to quench their vile plateau.
The sun sets ablaze, casting crimson light,
Upon a realm devoured by eternal night,
A twisted, eerie symphony resonates, resounds,
Knowing not peace nor solace, only death surrounds.
In this haunting land, where hope is consumed,
Life has turned to the bitter taste of doom,
Beware the animals, their monstrous guise,
For you may lose yourself, trapped in their eyes.

# XX

# Imperatrix

An empress forged in darkest thread
Within a realm of dystopian gaze
A kingdom bound in her twisted haze
She walks In the shattered dreams
Where light retreats and darkness teems
Her subjects whisper, hearts they cower
For in her grasp is their final hour
A chilling wind through corridors cold
Whispers tales that the darkness holds
In her eyes, a glint of cruel delight
Every threat, a reason to ignite

With piercing gaze and venomous dirge
She wields her power, an iron surge
Behind her mask, a heart laid bare
In crimson depths, no love to share

Each whispered rumor, a fate now sealed
Her subjects know not what's concealed
For in her chambers, secrets reside
Bound by fear, they choose to hide

They dare not rise, they dare not clash
She's woven chains, their spirits thrash
Her control a tempest, bloodied and true
Slaughtered meek, for they never knew
And as the moon descends upon despair
A chilling darkness fills the air
The empress smiles, claws unsheathed
Her subjects' fate, forever bequeathed
But in the silence, one voice does rise
A whispered truth, dispelling lies
A rebellion stirs, a seed of hope
From shadows born, refusing to cope
In hushed defiance, hearts ablaze
They seek to end her wicked maze
The empress trembles, control's mere ruse
An empire built on souls abused
But as time weaves its inky strain
n A sinister truth becomes more plain
For empires wrought on treacherous ground
Shall crumble beneath the victor's sound

In chilling battles, hope takes stand
United spirits, hand in hand
The empress falls, her empire breaks

Shattered dreams, compassion awakes
And so, as darkness finds its retreat
The chilling echoes of her defeat
A haunting tale through ages told
Of an empress cruel, by power ensnared and cold.

# XXI

=====

# Mirrored Illusion

I awaken from slumber, in a tormenting fright.
A nightmare so chilling, it pierced through my dreams,
Unleashing a darkness, a morbid extreme.
Seeking solace, I trudge to the kitchen's domain,
With trembling steps, this unease I disdain.
The yawn of the darkness, it twists and it churns,
As a chilling wind whispers, a lesson I must learn.

A flicker of hope ignites, as the light floods the room,
Dispelling the darkness that once held its gloom.
Yet, into the scene, a figure grotesque,
An identical twin, wearing a twisted burlesque.
Their visage like mine, an eerie reflection,
Grinning with malice, a twisted inception.
A knife gleaming coldly, a silver abyss,
Pointed at my being, a promise of darkness.

My pulse starts to quicken, my senses ensnared,
In this grim confrontation, where reality's impaired.
Are they truly a twin or a dark apparition?

A manifestation of my mind's grim composition.
Their laughter, a discordant melody of despair,
Piercing through my soul, an insidious snare.
The air becomes stagnant, heavy with dread,
As I stare into the eyes of the one who has bled.

In this wicked tableau, where nightmares collide,
I become entangled, with no place to hide.
A twisted reflection of my darkest desires,
Personified torment, a fantasy that fuels fires.
And as the night deepens, a symphony so grim,
The twin edges closer, darkness creeping within.
Will I succumb to this macabre inception?

Or awaken, and escape this dark reflection?
With resolve, I gather courage, my fear I defy
For a battle begins when the moon's on the sky.
The knife, like a serpent, poised to strike true,
But I'll fight for my essence, my spirit, my due.
I lunge without hesitation, my heart pounding fast,
Knowing it's a struggle, that my soul will outlast.
Steel clashes with steel, a dance in the abyss,
A battle of nightmares, sealed in this midnight tryst.

Through the haze of the nightmare, hope starts
to gleam, In this dark fantasy, a shadowed nightmare's
scheme.
I push through the anguish, reclaiming my core,
No longer a victim, but a conqueror of lore.
The twin, now a ghost, dissipates into shade,
As dawn's first light heralds a victory cascade.
Though shaken, I rise from this dark, eerie dance,
Embracing the light, with newfound resilience.
For in this morbid fantasy, a whispering decree,
That darkness must yield, when confronted, we see.
So remember this tale, when nightmares arise,
To face the reflection and claim your own prize.

# XXII

# Curiosity's Bane

In the midnight's shroud of malevolence,
A black horse carriage arrives, its presence dense,
Before your dwelling, a foreboding sight,
Whispers echo within the realm of night.
A gloved hand emerges from the abyss,
Inviting, mesmerizing, an enigmatic kiss,
Compelling doubts and fears to subside,
Bewitched, you embark, with fate to collide.
Stepping through the maw, a portal to unknown
, Within the carriage, shadows eerily grown,
Silent whispers fill the twisted air,
As darkness dances with a macabre flair.
Through realms uncharted, obscured by bleak
A journey sinister, the mind it seeks,
The horses' hooves pound against deadened earth,
As foreboding scents and ethereal sounds give birth.

Eyes peer from corners with hollow glare,
The carriage's essence, a surreal nightmare,
Thoughts entwined in spiraled dread,
In this twisted dark fantasy, terror is bred.

Through forests of haunt and tangled dreams,
Illusions weave, beckoning in gleeful fiends,
Echoes of anguish merge with ghostly cries,
A montage of torment, the mind's demise.

Gossamer whispers hiss within your ear,
Secrets concealed, the truth is unclear,
Questions unravel, weaving through your mind,
What fate awaits, in this dark design?
Beyond the realms of human plight,
Pandora's box reigns, released to ignite,
Your soul ablaze, entwined in the mire,

Engulfed by flames of this demonic pyre.
A tapestry of terror unfurls its tale,
Boundless nightmares, a haunting travail,
From the depths of subconscious yearning,
Provoking thoughts, relentlessly burning.

This black horse carriage, herald of doom,
Shrouded in darkness, far from salvation's bloom,
Now trapped within the spider's intricate lace,
You question your soul's journey through this twisted space.

But heed this caution, mortal soul,
For once you enter, relinquishing control,
You may forever linger in realms unknown,
A choice made lightly, but consequences sown.

# XXIII

---

# The Siren's Call

A woman wandered, lost and sere,
Searching for solace, love sincere,
Her trembling steps, both frail and weak,
Led her to a shop, mysterious and bleak.
Within its depths, a locket lay,
With whispers calling, she couldn't sway.
The lock of ancient silver fair,
Studded with onyx, burdened with despair,
A macabre pendant, tempting fate,
Unveiling mysteries and tempting hate.
Unknown to her, the horrors concealed,
The siren's voice, a pact was sealed.

With trembling hands, she clasped it tight,
Unveiling visions of deepest night.
Through eyes of wickedness, she beheld,

The thoughts of a killer, dark and compelled
. A song of madness, a wicked symphony,
Unleashed upon her spirit, a hellish harmony.

Within her mind, his voice did sing,
Of crimson rivers coursing free,
Of tortured souls, swiftly set free.
With oily whispers, he revealed his vice,
His twisted pleasures, drowned in ice.

With every heartbeat, the silence broke,
Her soul entwined, a morbid yoke,
She journeyed forth, her steps unsteady,
To trace the shadows, dark and heady.
Through barren lands, starved and bleak,
She followed the words his thoughts did speak.

A gallery of gore, a gruesome sight
, Each murder etched in shocking light.
In moonlit forests, where corpses lay,
She saw his victims, in disarray.
Their lifeless eyes, stared into her own,
Their vacant souls eternally prone.
Though terror sang within her core,
Curiosity forced her to explore,

Lost in the labyrinthine maze,
Chasing the echoes of his tormented ways.
Through blood-soaked halls devoid of glee,

She marched toward the depths of tragedy.

Terror laughed, as she succumbed,
To the essence of his darkness, she became numb.
Ethics faded, her conscience caved,
As she embraced the wicked path he paved.
An accomplice to his twisted dance,
She reveled in the depths of his malevolent trance.
No star could guide her, no light to find,

Only shadows taunting at her mind.
The siren's call, its melody surreal,
Engulfed her senses, consuming all she'd feel.
Her descent into madness, a foregone fate,
Bounded to the killer, forever sealed by hate.
In the end, when twisted tales converge,
When darkness melds and fates converge,
The locket's power, she had to sever,
The bond of evil, she'd endeavor.
But whispers lingered, as darkness gripped,
Forever haunted by the secrets she'd sipped.
So heed this tale, dear souls beware,
Of dark enchantments lurking there.
For in the depths of beauty's snare,
Lies the path to nightmares bare.
For when you seek the wicked gleam,
Remember, it may consume your dream.

# XXIV

# Infernal Waltz

In the depths of gloom, where shadows sway,
In a house bewitched, where ghosts hold sway,
Lies the tale of dread, where darkness would dwell,
A cursed melody, a haunting spell.
In the heart of night, when the moon hangs low,
A chilling waltz begins to flow,
From ebony keys, the notes start to rise,
An eerie tune, with a devilish guise.
A haunted specter, the piano's plea,
Awakens the souls that can never be free,
Their tortured voices, their torment cascades,
Mourning lost hopes and dreams that never fade.
Each night, the haunting chords resound,
In this accursed house, where spirits are bound,
Their phantom fingers, they dance on the keys,
A wicked ballet to whisper its decrees.

But on this fateful eve, the air turns bleak,
As the silence wraps its cold and suffocating sheen,
For the piano rests silent, the waltz is no more,
Unveiling the end from its age-old lore.
The heavens tremble, the stars lose their light,
As darkness descends, devouring the night,
The world swirls in chaos, souls cry in despair,
Transfixed in horror, it's a bitter nightmare.

The earth splits asunder, a chasm unfurls,
Revealing infernal flames, where salvation once twirled,
Creatures of abyss, now set free to roam,
Their feral hunger claiming blood as their own.
Beneath a blood-red sky, screams fill the air,
Echoes of agony, of hope turned to despair,
The Devil's Waltz, it played its final refrain,
A symphony of damnation, forever ordained.
In this realm of shadows, where darkness prevails,
The lost souls wander, dragged by invisible trails,
Haunted by the melody, eternally cursed,
No respite from torment, in this world unrehearsed.
So heed this warning, children of light,
Never venture near this house, plagued with night
, For once the music halts, and darkness unfurls,
The Infernal Waltz declares the end of the world.

# XXV

# The Timeless Clock

In forgotten depths where shadows waltz,
A tale of darkness through time unfolds,
Where a woman weaves in a cursed trance,
Bound by an old clock's desperate chance.
Within ancient halls, forlorn and bleak,
A legacy whispers, mystery to seek,
Inheritance bestowed upon her wary frame,

A timepiece of dread, her being to claim.
Midnight's embrace, a sinister chime,
Transcending beyond the bounds of time,
The cursed clock, its secrets untold,
Unveiling the darkness the past does hold.
With every tick, danger's breath draws near
, Through sinister portals, fueling her fear,
An enchantment bestowed, twisted and vile,

To witness crimes on earth's forsaken isle.
Through veils of woe, her journey persists
, To echoing screams, souls forever missed,
Across ages of sorrow, she is thrust,
A doomed witness in her relentless trust.

Doorways unravel, to eras corrupt,
Where violence marauds, to disrupt,
From medieval castles, stained and rife,
To blazing pyres, engulfed in strife.
The bloodied fields where battles were waged,
With life's essence spilt, malice uncaged,
A symphony of horrors, torment and woe,
Each era she visits, endless torment to sow.

Innocence shattered, hope's flickering wane
, She tiptoes through nightmares, soaked in pain,
A witness to torment, her soul left to fray,
Darkened impressions, haunting her each day.
Silent screams encircle her thoughts,
Haunted whispers of the crimes she's sought,
Through time's cruel grip, its relentless sting,
A fragile sanity clings to fraying string.
Her burdened soul, tendrils turned to ash,
A cloak of sorrow, a tormenting clash,
For with each journey, she pays a fee,
Her essence shattered, lost to eternity.

Yet through the horror, a yearning remains,

To uncover answers, to sever the chains,
To break the cycle, this harrowing plight,
And escape this eternal dance of fright.
For the cursed clock, a relic of death,
Holds secrets sacred, consuming each breath,
A woman, forever bound to its fate,

So she ventures forth, despite the toll,
On this twisted path, her salvation she'll enroll,

To banish the darkness, to end the despair,
To reclaim her life, and freedom's sweet air.
Thus, onward she marches, both brave and frail,
A sacrifice bound to this haunting tale,
A captive to time's malevolent grasp,
Searching for solace within shadows rasp.
In the tendrils of gloom, a glimmer of light,
A dim ember burning against endless night,
For within her soul, a flicker remains,
A testament to resilience, despite all pains.
And as she traverses the crimes of desolation,
With iron will and haunted determination
, She will rise above, this cyclical despair,
And conquer the clock's curse through endless prayer.

# XXVI

# Carnival of The Damned

In a quaint little town, snug and serene,
Where dreams were adorned with calm routine,
A carnival emerged in the dark of night,
Enchanting the souls with a whimsical bite.
Once a sleepy hamlet, peaceful and pure,
Now embraced by mystery, tales to lure,
A spectral eve arrived, mischief in the air,
As the midnight carnival debuts its flair.

With a flourish of stars and a whispering breeze,
The gates unlock, paving way for unease,
Twinkling lights danced through the velvety sky,
Announcing the arrival, the night let out a sigh.
In shadows stretching beyond the moon's glow,

The carnival bloomed, transforming the town below,

# XXVII

Arcane tents unfurled like the strangest of dreams,
Beckoning souls to enter, hear their silent screams.
From all walks of life, they ventured, entranced,
Boldly seeking the wonders fate had advanced,
Young and old, curiosity ablaze in their eyes,
Hopeful for tales spun under starlit skies.

By morn, the town awoke, mystery unfurled
, Obfuscating secrets, an illusionary world,
The carnival breathed whimsy, bright and thrilling,
A kaleidoscope of laughter, destiny fulfilling.

Gaily painted wagons, like rainbows at night,
Hushed whispers of stories, a bewitching sight,
Acrobats defying gravity with graceful sweep,
Jugglers taming chaos, laughter running deep.
Cotton candy clouds speckled the azure skies,
easing taste buds with nostalgic surprise,
Stilt walkers, enchanted, towered high above
, Their shadows trembled, harboring secrets of love.

But as golden hues faded, eve's curtain unfurled,
The carnival's true visage twisted and twirled,
From merry enchantment, a sinister bloom,
A masquerade of darkness, an unholy gloom.
A twisted ringmaster, grinning with malevolence,
His wicked eyes gleaming, harboring insolence,
Whispered promises of secrets never disclosed,
As the moon paled, the carnival's tale exposed.
The once dazzling rides lost their luster and light
, Their mechanical whimsy deformed by the night,
Delighting in fear, they laughed with eerie glee,
A dance of despair, a diabolical spree.
The carousel spun, horses galloping astray,
Feverish laughter echoed, haunting the bay,
Children's cries muffled, stolen by the abyss,
Innocence devoured by malevolent hiss.
The mirrors distorted, reflections torn asunder,
Distorted reflections, their souls left to wonder,
Twisted clowns cavorted, their grins full of spite,
Seeking laughter's anguish, infecting the night.

The carnival at night, a nightmarish abode,
A tapestry of horrors that torment and corrode,
Yet the townsfolk continued in morbid fascination,
Enthralled by the darkness, their souls' damnation.
For in the heart of this mystical carnival's plight,
Resided allure and a curious insight

A twisted reminder of the shadows we veil,
A playground for darkness, where one's fears prevail.
So tread lightly, dear traveler, through this carnival's snare,
And remember, nothing is as it seems in this nightmarish affair.
For it is within the heart of darkness that truths can unfurl,
In this macabre paradise, where dreams intertwine with the under-world.

# XXVIII

# Secrets of the Whispering Woods

Whispers echo, a mysterious retort.
Secrets of the past, present, and beyond,
A tapestry woven, each tale responds.
Beneath the boughs, where shadows conspire,
The trees whisper tales, a spectral choir.
Collective memories in leaves and bark,
A dialogue enigmatic, a woodland spark.
"Listen," they murmur, as the wind takes flight,
Guiding the traveler through the dappled light.
Stories of those who walked this hallowed ground,
Whispers of wisdom, in silence, profound.

The ancient oaks, guardians of time,
Speak of histories, a rhythm in rhyme.

Their branches, like arms, reach to embrace,
The wanderer seeking a tranquil space.

As footsteps tread on the mossy floor,
The secrets of the forest begin to pour.
Warnings of paths untrodden, unseen,
In the whispering woods, the truth lies between.

"Time is a river, ever flowing,
In the dance of life, ever unknowing.
Past, present, future entwine,
In the tapestry of nature's design."
Guidance offered in rustling leaves,
A dialogue that never deceives.
The mysteries of life, in shadows, concealed,
In the heart of the forest, truths revealed.
The traveler, an audience to the arboreal song,
As the whispering woods unravel the throng
Of stories entwined with roots and streams,
Nature's dialogue, a bridge of dreams.

So, in the embrace of the whispering trees,
Find solace, wisdom, and mysteries.
For in the forest's murmurs, the soul understood,
The timeless refrain of the whispering wood.

# XXIX

# Dance of the Marionettes

There lies a twisted tale, a realm of shattered dreams,
Where life and death entwine, painted with gruesome schemes.
Once, an empire thrived, under a puppeteer's control,
A master of illusion, with secrets he did hold,
His marionettes, crafted with delicate art,
Conveyed stories untold, played from his heart.

Each night, curtains unveiled, the theater would ignite,
As wood hummed, thread shimmered, like souls taking flight,
In this twisted spectacle, twisted was the theme,

A haunting performance, a macabre, wicked dream.
It was whispered, the puppeteer, a man of might and grace,

A sorcerer of politics, his maneuvers interlaced
But lurking 'round the corner, in alleyways concealed,
Stalked shadowed figures, knives at their will revealed.

One fateful eve, whispers revealed his demise,
Unsolved, an unseen act, veiled by cloudy skies,

Yet with each twilight's fall, a mystic spell unwound,
His marionettes awoke, silently on the ground.

They danced in empty halls, a spectral waltz imbued,
Reenacting his death, the crime that wasn't subdued,
The melody of strings, woven with spectral grace,
Their movements filled with sorrow, pain etched on their face.
The puppeteer's phantom, in crimson-stained attire,
His voice echoed through the void, stoking every fire,
Reciting tainted verses of power and deceit,
His essence forever trapped, in shadows bittersweet.

The puppets, bound by strings, acted out his fate,
Each night a twisted play, replaying his cruel date,
Swords plunged through the air, in a macabre ballet,
Ethereal screams resounded, as they reenacted the slay.
In this theater of the damned, in twisted wood and thread,
The marionettes danced, portraying the master's dread,
Haunting political overtones twisted their play,
Echoing suppressed truths, concealed within their display.

The first was the King, a tyrant unjust
His greed knew no bounds, his heart filled with lust,
The puppet's strings tangled, as he met his fate,
Betrayed by his own, consumed by his own hate.

Next came the Queen, a puppet of desire,
Her beauty enchanting, her soul engulfed in fire,
Her emerald eyes, wrought with deceit,
Unveiled before all, her poisonous deceit.

Then came the General, a puppet fierce and bold,
But treasonous thoughts within his heart took hold,
His blade turned against him, stained red with his doom
A puppet once valiant, brought down by his own tomb.
The puppets danced, their strings intertwining,
With mournful music, their souls reclining,
Their master's tragedy, forever suspended
In each haunting performance, their pain never ended.
The nobles watched in fear, their masks tightly worn,
Secrets losing their grip, as destiny was reborn,
For the marionettes whispered tales only they knew,
Unveiling oppressive truths, across the empire they flew.

A symphony of nightmares, a tapestry of pain,
The puppeteer, a martyr, forevermore to remain,
Yet the puppets danced with purpose, with each chilling verse,
Injustice in each step, a plea to lift the curse.

But shadows can't be slain, for they forever roam,
And the puppeteer's legacy engulfed their fated home,
His marionettes, trapped in eternal sorrow, sublime,
Forever cursed to recreate his murder in endless time.

# XXX

# The Weeping Statue

Beneath the moon's somber glow, a churchyard stood,
Where a statue wept tears of blood
With its hallowed stone face, chiseled in despair
, It stood tall in silence, all secrets laid bare.
Carved long ago, when kings and queens were young,
It held a curse within, a tragedy unsung.
Each full moon's rise brought forth a gruesome sight,
As blood trickled from its eyes, covering the night.
Witnessing such turmoil, a city's heart would quake,
For the statue's curse was more than anyone could take.
The land, engulfed in chaos, drowned in sorrow's sea,
As blood-soaked tears fell, destroying unity.
Whosoever gazed upon this twisted shrine,
Became a living effigy, cursed by fate malign.
From peasants to nobles, the curse would not discriminate,
No matter one's wealth, all suffered the same fate.

Whispered falsehoods danced in shadows dark and deep,
As each victim's demise brought more anguish to reap.
The priest, a cunning man with wicked desires,
Saw opportunity in the weeping statue's fires.
He preached to the masses, his words an intricate spell,
A calculated manipulation, diabolic, and unwell.
He claimed the statue's tears would protect the realm,
From enemies abroad, plotting their overwhelming overwhelm.
But behind his hollow words, a sinister pact was sealed,
He sought power and control, his hunger unconcealed.

One by one, the innocent fell into despair,
Transformed into statues, frozen in a life unfair.
The priest, now a tyrant, ruled with an iron fist,
Feasting upon the curses, his position he would persist.
Yet within the crumbling walls of desolation and pain,
A glimmer of hope emerged, a beacon to regain.
A secret resistance, hidden under moon's guise,

Determined to uncover the truth, beneath the priest's lies.
They unearthed the dark past, the statue's haunting tale,
A legend of betrayal, where innocence would fail.
A love betrayed, a sacrifice condemned by greed,
Causing the statue's curse, a legacy that would bleed.
With knowledge in their hands, they rallied the oppressed,
A rebellion in motion, no longer to be repressed.

They stormed the churchyard, as blood moon ascended high,

The priest's reign of darkness would crumble, by and by.
In the final showdown, blood and steel danced in the air,
As the statue's weeping tears mingled, becoming aware.
With justice as their weapon, the resistance fought,
Their valor and determination, a testament never to be forgot.

And as the statue's curse, finally lifted its chains,
The priest's wicked reign faded, the land washed of its stains
. No longer weeping, the statue reflected a new dawn,
A reminder that power's chains can forever be undone

# XXXI

# The Hourglass Shatters

## Gallery of the Broken

In this gallery of shattered dreams,
Each piece never quite what it seems.
Whispers of what could have been,
Lost hopes and wishes left unseen.

The first painting, a portrait of love,
Two souls intertwined, high above.
Embracing in a timeless dance,
But now just a memory, left to chance.

A sculpture of a child's laughter,
Frozen in time, what came after?
Innocence lost, dreams crushed by reality,
A fleeting moment of pure vitality.
An installation of forgotten glory,
Promises made, the end of the story.
Ambitions high, now fallen low,

A mirror reflecting the ebb and flow.

A canvas of a world at peace,
Where conflicts cease, and worries cease.

But the brushstrokes tell a different tale,
Of discord and anguish that prevail.

As you wander through this solemn space,
Contemplate each dream's final trace.
The beauty in the broken hopes,
The resilience in the shattered ropes.
For in these fragments of what could be,
Lies the essence of humanity.
The struggle, the loss, the bittersweet
, In every broken dream we meet.
Time's shadow stretches, an eternal flight.
A tangible presence, a relentless stream,
Enveloping all in its ceaseless dream.
A cloak draped over moments, both near and far,
Time's shadow whispers of who we are.
It weaves through lives, a silent guide,
Marking the ebb and flow of the tide.

In the tapestry of existence, it threads,
A narrative of beginnings and of the sheds.
A legacy imprinted on history's wall,
In the silent footsteps that echo and call.
As the sun rises and the shadows wane,

Time's touch paints with hues of joy and pain.
Moments of clarity, like the noonday sun,

Reveal the tales that time has spun.
Yet, shadows linger, even in the day,
A reminder that moments slip away.
The interplay of light and darkness unfolds,
As time's story, in every heartbeat, molds.
Societies rise and civilizations fall,
Under time's shadow, a common thrall.
A silent witness to the rise and decay,
It marks the passage of every day.

Through the cycles of dawn and dusk,
Time's shadow weaves its intricate musk.
In obscurity, it shrouds the unknown,
In clarity, the seeds of wisdom are sown.
Omnipresent, it knows no bound,
A cosmic dance, silent and profound.
In the corridors of fate and chance,
Time's shadow weaves its cosmic dance.
So, let us embrace the fleeting light,
In the face of time's relentless flight.

# XXXII

# Kaleidoscope

Drifting along a winding path where shadows weep,
Lost souls wander, their secrets to keep.
A perilous journey, not just in stride,
Grappling with loss, they step in the gloom,
Aching hearts searching for a healing bloom.
Uncertainty looms, like a shroud in the air,
Yet, the path unfolds, challenging despair.
Each step a struggle, a silent plea,
Lost souls yearning to break free.
The echoes of their footsteps, a mournful song,
As they navigate a journey both arduous and long. T
he path is lined with thorns of regret,
Yet, hope flickers, a dim silhouette.

Through the mist of tears and the fog of doubt,
Lost souls find strength, their essence devout.

In the labyrinth of anguish, a quest for meaning,
They confront the shadows, their own hearts cleaning
. The path reveals truths, both bitter and sweet,
As lost souls dance with destiny, their fate to meet
Challenges arise like mountains to climb,
Yet, resilience blooms in the fullness of time.
The path teaches lessons, profound and deep,
As lost souls awaken from a restless sleep.
Yet within the struggles, revelations gleam,
Like stars in the night sky, a radiant beam.
For in the journey of the lost and pained,
New perspectives are gained, wisdom attained.
The path may twist, and the road may wind,
But lost souls, in unity, strength they find.
Through the valleys of despair, and peaks of hope,
So, let the winds of healing gently blow,
As lost souls journey, let empathy grow.
In the tapestry of emotions, a story unfolds,
Of lost souls finding solace as their tale molds.

# XXXIII

# Decaydence

In the ballet of decay, a silent waltz,
Nature's dance, a transformative assault.
A slow, graceful pirouette in the still air,
Decay unfolds, a dance beyond compare.
Leaves of autumn, once vibrant and bold,

Now crumble and fade in a tapestry old.
The dance of decay in the forest's embrace,
Breaking down the past, creating space.

Abandoned places, echoes of time,
Whispers of stories, a nostalgic chime.
The dance unfolds in crumbling walls,
A graceful surrender, as the old recalls.

Eerie beauty in the moss-covered stone,

As decay claims kingdoms, yet stands alone.
A dance of transformation, relentless and sure,
Decay whispers of beginnings obscure.
In personal decline, a poignant ballet,
A metamorphosis in the fading gray.

Lines on the face, etched by years,
The dance of decay, shedding old fears.
Yet, within the decay, a secret is spun,
A dance of rebirth, a new day begun.
The old gives way to the sprout of green,
In the dance of decay, a cycle unseen.
The rust on iron, the weathered wood,
A dance that reflects both misunderstood.
For in the breaking down, a rebirth is found,
A paradoxical dance on life's sacred ground.

Ephemeral beauty in the crumbling art,
As decay's dance plays a vital part.
A reminder that all things find their end,
To nurture the soil for what's around the bend.

So, let the dance unfold, eerie and grand,
Decay's ballet, a cosmic command.
In the rhythm of breakdown, a silent chance,
For new beginnings in the dance of decay's trance

# XXXIV

# Earthbound

Forgotten people, their tales untold,
Extinct languages, like secrets, unfold.
Silenced opinions, a hushed refrain,
In this spectral chamber, their echoes remain.
What stories would these voices share,
If the present were willing to hear?
A symphony of wisdom, warnings profound,
lost voices echoing, a haunting sound.
"Remember," cries an ancient tongue,
From the abyss where echoes are flung.
A chorus of spirits, yearning to impart,
The lore of ages, a ghostly art.
Warnings of wars, forgotten lore,
Echoes of tragedies from times of yore.
In the realm where time and echoes entwine,
Lost voices linger, a spectral sign.

"Listen," they murmur in spectral plea,
To tales of resilience and agony.
Whispers of love and battles won,
Lost voices speak of what's done and undone.
The wisdom of sages, the innocence of youth,
Echoes of justice, whispers of truth.
Yet, in this dark, evocative abyss,
The echoes lament what the present might miss.

In the tapestry woven by voices lost,
A narrative haunting, a spectral cost.
As the echoes linger, the present entwines,
With the voices that time left behind.
So, let us listen to the ghostly cries,
To the echoes of voices that never dies.

For in their haunting, a lesson we find,
The lost voices, a bridge through time.

# XXXV

# Aeternitas

They dance and wither as time defies.
Spring, a seductress with petals fair,
Blooms in lust, entwining in the air.
But beneath the blossoms, a dark intent,
A fleeting dalliance, soon to be spent.
As spring entices with fragrant deceit,
The withering whispers, a tale replete.

Summer strides with fiery might,
A blaze of passion, a searing light.
Yet, within the heat, a subtle decay,
The vibrant hues slowly fade away.
Autumn's melancholy, a mournful wail,
Leaves cascading in a somber gale.
The beauty lies in the impending doom,
A dance of death in nature's ballroom.

Winter emerges, a cold embrace,
A desolate canvas, a chilling space.
Silent stillness, a frozen abyss,

As life surrenders to winter's kiss.
Each season a mask, a fleeting grace,
A twisted ballet, a spectral chase.
The cycle of life, a sinister rhyme,
As seasons wither in the hands of time.
In their demise, reflections appear,
Echoes of joy and sorrow, crystal clear.
The transient beauty of a world in decay,
Mirroring the human experience's disarray.
So, behold the withering seasons' tale,
A darkened ballet, an ephemeral trail.
In their passing, a reminder cold,
That beauty and decay, a story old.

# XXXVI

# Refrain

Moments pass, a whisper in the air,
Leaving imprints on the soul laid bare.
The taste of joy, a bittersweet wine,
A sip of ecstasy, a moment divine.
Yet, like the waning moon in the night,
Fleeting joy slips away from our sight.

A memory lingers, a haunting ghost,
A reminder of the joy we once boasted.
Sorrow, a mistress with a somber grace,
Leaves her mark in the heart's hollow space.
Her touch, a dagger, sharp and cold,
A moment's weight, a story untold.
Revelation, a seductress in disguise,
Opens the gates to the soul's uncharted skies.
In a fleeting gaze, a truth is unveiled,

Leaving the heart and mind enraptured, impaled.

These moments, like phantoms, come and go,
Leaving footprints in the sands we sow.
Their weight profound, their significance clear
, Fleeting moments shape the essence we hold dear.
In the dance of time, a relentless tide,
Fleeting moments in which we confide.
They mold our thoughts, our actions, our being,
A kaleidoscope of life, ever-seeing.
So, in the darkness where shadows weave,
Embrace the moments, let them deceive.
For in their fleeting grasp, a lifetime unfolds

# XXXVII

# Phobos

Living nightmares emerge from the darkness, unbowed.
Tangible fears take shape in the still of the night,
Confronting individuals in a harrowing plight.
Shadowy figures with eyes that gleam,
Haunt the waking world like a chilling dream.
Whispers of dread in the midnight air,
As nightmares weave their intricate snare.
Shapes shift and morph in the veil of night,

Manifestations of the subconscious in eerie light.
From twisted visions to echoing screams,
Nightmares pierce the veil of dreams.

A phantasmagoria of horrors untold,
Unraveling fears in a narrative bold.
From the depths of the psyche, they arise,

Reflecting the truth hidden behind lies.

In the waking world, their presence lingers,
A spectral dance, like skeletal fingers.

The line between reality and nightmare blurred,
As the veil of night is slowly stirred.

Yet, with the dawn, comes a glimmer of hope,
A reprieve from the nightmares' cruel scope.
As sunlight banishes the shadows deep,
The living nightmares retreat, in fitful sleep.
But dusk approaches with apprehension anew,
As the veil descends, the nightmares renew.
In the intersection of reality and dread,
The nightmares linger, in whispers unsaid.

So, in the darkness where fears take flight,
Remember the dawn will bring respite.
But under the veil of night, the subconscious reigns
, And living nightmares haunt the mind's domain

In a chamber dim where shadows wade,
A mirror stands, a truth cascade.
Not just a reflection of the skin,
But the innermost thoughts, a world within.
Gazing into the glass, a silent plea,
The mirror reveals what the soul can't flee.
Thoughts laid bare, fears unfurled,

A confrontation with the inner world.

In the silvered surface, a relentless gaze,
Echoes of desires in a silent blaze.
The mirror speaks in truths untold,
A symphony of secrets, a tale to unfold.
Fears rise like specters in the night,
Dancing in the mirror's unyielding light.
Confrontation with the shadows cast,
A journey into the soul's vast vast.
Acceptance blooms like a fragile flower,
In the reflective embrace of the mirrored bower.

Yet, fear may grip, an iron hand,

As the mirror unveils the heart's own land.
A quest for change may stir the soul,
As revelations play and take their toll.
In the dance of reflection, a paradox found,
A mirror that echoes, without a sound.
The complexities of self in the mirrored frame,
For in the glass, a truth profound,

A journey of self-discovery unbound.
So, in the mirror's gaze, what will you see?
A confrontation with your own mystery.
Acceptance, fear, or a quest for change,
In the reflective dance, the self may rearrange

# XXXVIII

# To Cast Aside The Chains

Invisible chains bind, a subjugated strand.
Societal expectations, silent and tight,
Personal fears that constrict the light.
Forged in whispers and unspoken decree

These chains define, yet none can see.
A labyrinth of obligations, a web entwined,
Around the heart, the soul confined.
From birth, they form, a subtle restraint

Unseen shackles, silent and quaint.
Threads of conformity, woven with care,
Invisible chains, a burden to bear.
The struggle begins, a silent fight

Against the chains that grip so tight.
To break the bonds, to find release,
To let the spirit and soul find peace.
The forge of freedom, a fiery quest
Against the chains, a heart's protest.

Unraveling threads of societal mold,
To rediscover the authentic, the untold.
Courage is the hammer, resilience the flame

Against the invisible chains, a daring claim.
The journey is arduous, the path unclear
But liberation whispers, ever near.
To break free, one must first believe,
In the power to change, to unweave.

To challenge norms, to rise above,
The invisible chains that bind and shove.
In the struggle against the unseen weight
, Liberation comes, albeit late.
Breaking free from the silent strife,

A dance with freedom, a renewed life.
For in the shadows where chains entwine
, Courage blooms, a light divine.
The strength to shatter the silent refrain,
To break the invisible chains that restrain
In the landscape of the mind, a tempest brews,

A turbulent storm, where thoughts confuse.
Thunderous roars echo through the expanse,
As the storm within takes its fervent chance.
Clouds of confusion, emotions collide,
In the stormy depths where chaos resides.
Lightning strikes of anger, fierce and bright,
Illuminate the tumult, a tempest's fright.
Torrential rains, a deluge of tears,
A downpour of sorrows, washing fears.
The storm within, a relentless cascade,
A chaotic dance, a tempest charade.
Winds of doubt, howling through the mind

Twisting and turning, unyielding, unkind.
The tempest's escalation, a rising tide,
As inner turmoil refuses to subside.
At the peak, a crescendo of despair,
A whirlwind of thoughts tearing through the air.
Conflicting emotions, a turbulent sea,
In the stormy landscape where chaos is free.

Yet, in the heart of the tempest's might,
A paradox emerges, a beacon of light.
Catharsis whispers through thunderous din,

A transformative process about to begin.
As the storm exhausts its fervent spree,
A calm descends over the internal sea.
The tempest's chaos begins to wane,

Leaving behind a cleansed, tranquil terrain.
In the aftermath, a silent rebirth,
A calm after chaos, a serene hearth.
The storm within, once fierce and wild,
Now subdued, like the tranquil after the storm filed.

# XXXIX

# Garden of Reminiscence

In a garden where time takes root,
Eras blossom, a historical pursuit.
Each plant a story, vibrant or worn,
A tapestry of lessons, a garden adorned.

Ancient blooms with petals of gold,
Representing stories from days of old.
Lessons in wisdom, echoes profound,
In the garden where history is found.

Medieval buds in armor of green,
Chivalry and strife in the scene.
A tale of knights, a clash of might,
In the garden of time, a medieval sight.

Renaissance flowers, a burst of art,

Creativity blooming, a masterpiece's start.
Lessons of rebirth, in colors untold,
In the garden where tales of the
Renaissance unfold.

Baroque blossoms, ornate and grand,
A symphony of opulence, a rich demand.
Lessons of excess, in petals wide,
In the garden where Baroque flowers bide.
Enlightenment vines, reaching for the sky,
Ideas like tendrils, spreading high.
Lessons of reason, of minds set free,
In the garden where
Enlightenment blooms decree.

Industrial stems with gears of steel,
A revolution turning, with a relentless zeal.
Lessons of progress, and its shadowed side,
In the garden where Industrial blooms confide.

Modern buds in a chaotic array,
Technological petals in the light of day.
Lessons of change, of the fast-paced kind,
In the garden where Modern flowers find.

Postmodern tendrils, a complex weave,
A garden of ideas that interleave.
Lessons of deconstruction, a postmodern show,
In the garden where ideas ebb and flow.

Cyclical is the nature of this garden grand,
A continuum of time, forever planned.
Lessons in growth, in decay, in bloom,
In the garden where history finds room.

So, walk through this garden, each era in view,
Hear the whispers of lessons old and new.
For in the cyclical nature of this rhyme,
Lies the wisdom of the garden, the heartbeat of time

# XL

---

# Discard The Masks//Cutthroat Masquerade

In the masquerade of life, a dance of veils,
Masks adorned to hide the tales.
A symphony of faces, each a disguise,
Concealing truths in a world of lies.

Reasons myriad, behind the masks we wear,
To fit the molds society lays bare.
Conformity's pressure, a weight to bear,
As authenticity hides in the masked affair.

Masks of strength to shield the soul,
Concealing vulnerabilities, making us whole.

Yet, behind the facade, the truth peeks through,
A glimpse of authenticity, a moment true.

Wearing masks to blend, to belong,

In the crowd where echoes of masks prolong.
A complex dance in a masked ballet,
As identities shift and sway.
But what is lost when masks persist,
In the quest for approval, authenticity dismissed?
Moments arise when masks may slip,
Revealing the soul, an unscripted script.
In vulnerability, a beauty found,
As the mask falls to the silent ground.
A search for authenticity, a quest to be real,
In the masked world, a genuine appeal.

Yet, in the mirror of society's gaze,
Masks persist in a relentless blaze.
For authenticity, a courageous fight,
In the masked masquerade of day and night.

So, let us ponder the masks we don,
The reasons behind, the battles won.

# XLI

# The Gears of Fate

In the clockwork of fate, a dance unseen,
Cogs in motion, lives caught in between.
Predestined paths, a cosmic design,
Yet, whispers of free will in the grand design.
Each life, a cog in the vast machine,

Turning and churning, part of the routine.
Threads of destiny, tightly wound,
In the clockwork of fate, a chorus unbound.
Feelings entangled in the gears of time,
A struggle for autonomy, a subtle climb.
Believing in a plan, predetermined and grand,
Yet yearning for choices, free and unplanned.

In the clockwork of fate, emotions swell,
A symphony of lives, each a story to tell.

The illusion of choice, a bittersweet song,
As the gears of destiny grind along.
Questions arise in the quiet of the night,
Are we actors or merely a scripted sight?
In the vast machinery of fate's embrace,

Is there room for freedom, for a personal grace?

The struggle for meaning in the clockwork's hum
, Autonomy versus destiny, a beat on the drum.
Yearning to break free from the invisible hand,
To forge our own paths in the cosmic sand.
Yet, in the clockwork, a paradox unfolds,
Choices made, and destinies foretold.
A delicate dance, a cosmic ballet,
In the intricate clockwork, we find our way.
So, ponder the balance of choice and fate,
In the clockwork's rhythm, where lives conflate.
For in the grand design of destiny's art,
We navigate the cogs, each playing our part.
In the aftermath of war, a haunting silence reigns
, Echoes of violence in the scars that remain.
Not just in the rubble and ruins left behind,
But in the shadows that linger in the human mind.

Unhealed wounds, both seen and unseen,
A legacy of pain where hope once had been.
The physical scars, a testament to strife,
But the psychological toll cuts deeper than a knife.

In the eyes of survivors, a haunted gaze,
Memories of horror that time cannot erase.
The weight of loss, the burden of grief,
In the aftermath of war, there is no relief.

Societies torn apart, fractured and torn
, In the aftermath of conflict, hope is worn.
Divisions deepen, trust shattered and frayed,
As the echoes of violence refuse to fade.
Generations inherit the trauma of the past,
Caught in the shadow of war's lasting cast.
The stories untold, the pain passed down,

A legacy of suffering that knows no bounds.
In the silence of remembrance, we bear witness
, To the enduring shadow of war's darkness.
But even within the deepest sorrow, there is a flicker of light,
In the resilience of the human spirit's fight.
For even in the aftermath of the darkest hour,
There is strength in solidarity, in the will to empower.
And though the scars may never fully heal,
We find solace in the bonds that we feel.
So let us remember, and let us strive,
To honor the fallen and the survivors' drive.
For in the shadow of war, we find the strength
to endure, And in unity, we find hope for a future pure.

# XLII

# Time's Reprisal

Whispers linger, the silent moans.
Remnants of civilizations lost to time,
Echoes of stories, a rhythm sublime.
Dust of ages veils the tales,
Of thriving cultures, now mere trails.
Through crumbling archways, shadows play,
A dance of memories in the light's decay.
Artifacts in the soil, silent and still,
Hold the secrets that time distills.
Cities that once touched the sky,
Now reduced to remnants, where echoes lie.
Wandering through the ruins' embrace,
Feeling the heartbeat of a bygone race.
Lost civilizations, voices unheard,
In the poetry of relics, their stories stirred.
Once vibrant markets, now silence pervades,

Where laughter danced in colonnades.
What led to their downfall, lost in the mist,
Buried in the layers that time has kissed.
Lessons hidden in the fallen walls,
Tales of triumphs and tragic falls.
Civilizations that rose and then were gone,
Their legacy lingers, a silent dawn.
Temples that crumble, their gods long gone,
Yet, the spirit of worship lingers on.
Lessons of hubris, of rise and decline,
In the remnants of a lost design.
Wandering through the echoes of the past,
In the dust of ages, memories cast.
These remnants breathe tales of might,
A testament to the ebb and flow of light.
So, listen closely as the wind sighs,
Through the ruins where history lies.
For in the echoes of civilizations lost,
Are lessons and stories, a price and a cost.
In the vessel of existence, an hourglass turns,
Sands slipping through, as the universe yearns.
Each grain, a moment, a heartbeat's chime,
In the relentless flow of the river of time.
From the top to the bottom, an eternal race,
Life's tapestry woven in the hourglass's embrace.
Beginnings and endings, a cyclical song,
Moments captured, then swiftly gone.
The top bulb, a cradle of new-born light,
The bottom, a repository where shadows alight

. The journey of a soul, from birth to decay,
In the hourglass's dance, the mortal ballet.
The sands whisper tales of joy and sorrow,
Of dreams pursued, and a hopeful tomorrow.
Yet, as the grains cascade in the glass,
They slip through fingers, a transient pass.
Moments fleet, like butterflies in flight,
In the hourglass, a symphony of day and night.
The realization of mortality, a bittersweet truth,
In the grains of sand, the fountain of youth
. As the last grain falls with a muted sound,
Does it mark an end, a silence profound?
Or does it signal a passage to the unknown,
A realm where the seeds of the soul are sown?
Beyond the hourglass, a mystery untold,
A destination where tales of life unfold.
The sands may vanish, but what remains,
Are echoes of laughter and heartful refrains.
So, let us ponder the hourglass's lore,
As time's river flows forevermore.

## Gambling With Fate

Where the stale scent of spilled spirits lingers,
And the timeworn walls echo with whispered secrets,
A congregation of ancient gods has gathered,
Their immortal presence casting an ominous shadow.
They convene in a clandestine corner, obscured from mortal
eyes,

Their divine countenances veiled in the dim, smoky haze,

As they indulge in a timeless game of chance and consequence,

Poker chips of cosmic significance clinking and clattering,

Within the ethereal cadence of their celestial laughter.

Here, within the mortal realm, they wager more than gold,

Their bets transcending the trivial pursuits of humankind,

Smashed pint glasses become symbols of discord and upheaval,

Freak snowstorms, pawns in their enigmatic machinations,

And in a chilling twist, my very name becomes a bargaining chip.

I, a mere mortal, find myself unwittingly entwined,

In the fabric of their unfathomable game,

My essence becoming a token in their divine gamble,

As the gods manipulate the threads of destiny and chance,

Dealing fate like a deck of cards in the palm of their omnipotent hands.

The pub throbs with an otherworldly energy,

As the gods wield their influence with an air of ancient authority,

The stakes escalating with each turn of the cosmic deck,

My existence hanging precariously in the balance of their wager.

# XLIII

# Twinkie's Game

Twinkie, my little cat, wandering worlds in-between,
Her gaze a void, a sight unseen,
Her bi-colored fur ripples in the grip of unseen hands,
A spectral dance in unearthly lands.
Her voice, a troublemaker's caterwaul,
Shattering the silence of night,
A dissonant melody, a haunting sight,
Twisting, contorting in impossible forms,
Caught in a dance of spectral norms.
In the half-light, she babbles of realms untold,
Of secrets whispered, of mysteries to unfold,
Then in a blink, she's speeding away once more,
Mischief's adventurer playing on a spectral shore.
Twinkie, a creature of chaotic disarray,
Racing full-tilt through the echoes of a disjointed play,
Between the realms of here and there,

A phantom presence, haunting the air.

# XLIV

# Loaded Dice

The dice, an enigmatic oracle, held sway,
Revealing not chance, but a twisted design,
Each roll a harbinger of fate's capricious hand.
The number unveiled, a portentous omen,
A cipher for the impending tide of events,
A countdown to peril, or a shield of calculated deceit,
Unraveling the tapestry of clandestine machinations.
In its unyielding faces, the dice mirrored the stakes,
A silent witness to the dance of shadows and secrets,
Unveiling the count of approaching sentinels,
Or the fabric of untruths to be spun.
In its unfathomable language, it dictated the tempo,
A metronome of impending danger, a grim conductor,
Tallying the heartbeat of impending doom,
Or the fleeting moments before the echo of gunfire.

# XLV

# Parasite

In this house, another lurks, unseen by light,
Through cracks and keyholes, its secrets unfurl,
A specter within, shrouded in the depths of night.
Unfamiliar rooms beckon, beyond my sight,
Obscured by hinges, they taunt and swirl,
In this house, another lurks, unseen by light.
Dark red walls exude an eerie might,
Whispers of hunger, an insidious pearl,
A specter within, shrouded in the depths of night.
Emptiness echoes, a sinister plight,
A parasitic hunger, a clandestine twirl,
In this house, another lurks, unseen by light.
I navigate the maze, a perilous flight,
Haunted by the house's enigmatic swirl,
A specter within, shrouded in the depths of night.
Elusive and silent, evading my sight,

The second house, a mystery, a cryptic whirl,
In this house, another lurks, unseen by light

# XLVI

# Cursed

My neighbors are whispering about a forgotten legend,
A tale of darkness that lies within the woods' core,
Their hushed tones linger, haunting my restless nights,
As chilling winds howl, carrying secrets I knew not,
Fear grips my heart, for I sense the truth in those cries,
A forgotten power awakens, unseen yet ever so true.
In shadows' depths, I venture, consumed by the legend,
Seeking answers, beneath the veil of the forest's core,
Eyes wide and wary, I listen to the mournful cries,
Caught between realms of reality and all that's not,
Within eerie glow, I glimpse the secrets I once knew,
Lured deeper into darkness, longing for peaceful nights.
Each day, the sun descends, surrendering to the night,
Where whispers grow louder, fueled by dread and legend,
My sanity wavers, remembering what I once knew,
Buried beneath layers of forgotten tales at the core,

Its tendrils entwined, a web spun from illusions not,
Yet the cries persist, in echoes that remain ever true.
As darkness thickens, shadows dance throughout the night,
Gnawing at my thoughts, with whispers veiled in deceit and not,
Their haunting melodies blur the lines of myth and legend,
I strive to decipher, to uncover what lies at the core,
But the more I strive, the further I'm led from what's true,
Engulfed in despair, I'm lost in the abyss I once knew.
Beneath a moonless sky, my soul wrestles with what's true,
Haunted by visions, in the abyss that encompasses the night,
The truth eludes me, as I search for what I surely knew,
The whispers now a symphony, its melodies fierce and not,
The forest reveals its secrets, locking me in its core,
Immortalized in its grasp, I become part of this legend.
A crown of thorns rests on my brow, as I become the legend,
A prisoner to the knowledge, forever cursed to know what's true,
Transfixed, I find solace, trapped at the forest's core,
Embracing the darkness, I yearn for endless night,
For in the depths lies freedom, a release from what's not,
A whispered memory, now lost, but once dear and knew.
My neighbors cease their whispers, the legend now known,
Forever entwined with darkness, my destiny ever true,
In the woods, I'll reside, where the cries echo each night.

# XLVII

**It Wasn't Supposed To End Like This**

It wasn't supposed to end like this...

I apologized and pulled the trigger...

I opened my eyes and everything was dark...

Her heart stopped beating, but her eyes blinked open...

The smell of blood overwhelmed me...

The screams came from all around me...

I tried to run, but it pulled me in...

The fear in my gut grew as the laughing got louder...

The abandoned mansion called to me...

After an hour of waiting, I could no longer hear him...

The truck wouldn't stop following me...

Something about their faces sent shivers down my spine...

The boat came closer, but no one was on it...

The soft voice came from somewhere inside...

If it wasn't me, then who was it...

We needed more time, but time was up...

The temperature was rising and there was nowhere to go...

The hole opened under me, and I fell in...

Once the gate opened, there was no going back...

There was no one left when the game was done…
Everyone had left and I had no one to help now…
It was the end of everything, and that was only the beginning…
Monsters were only in stories, but this was real…
I turned the light on, and what I saw haunted me…
It was time to sleep, but I knew it'd be back…